# LIFE CYCLE OF A GOAT

### by Noah Leatherland

Minneapolis, Minnesota

**Credits**

All images are courtesy of Shutterstock.com, unless otherwise specified. With thanks to Getty Images, Thinkstock Photo, Adobe Stock, and iStockphoto. Cover – photomaster, Borodatch, Olga1818, Eric Isselee. Recurring images – Konde Hipe, uiliaaa, YummyBuum, tanyaya, Terdpong, wannawit_vck, summer studio. 2 – ShotPrime Studio, Ross Gordon Henry. 4–5 – Dernkadel, NIKS ADS, Visual Wings, Ami Parikh, Prostock-studio, Gods_Kings, IndianFaces. 6–7 – Andrew Mayovskyy, Aggie 11. 8–9 – ABC photographs, Ross Gordon Henry. 10–11 – hansgeel, Rita_Kochmarjova, Tanya May. 12–13 – Erika Norris, XPRZY. 14–15 – Branislav Cerven, ShotPrime Studio. 16–17 – Sharon Haeger, Robert Schneider, Esin Deniz, kolesnikovserg. 18–19 – Orphi Eulenforst, LiAndStudio. 20–21 – Lugres, Matej Kastelic. 22–23 – Inna Astakhova, Eric Isselee, nigel baker photography.

**Bearport Publishing Company Product Development Team**

Publisher: Jen Jenson; Director of Product Development: Spencer Brinker; Managing Editor: Allison Juda; Editor: Cole Nelson; Associate Editor: Naomi Reich; Associate Editor: Tiana Tran; Designer: Kim Jones; Designer: Kayla Eggert; Designer: Steve Scheluchin; Production Specialist: Owen Hamlin

Library of Congress Cataloging-in-Publication Data is available at www.loc.gov or upon request from the publisher.

ISBN: 979-8-89577-015-3 (hardcover)
ISBN: 979-8-89577-446-5 (paperback)
ISBN: 979-8-89577-132-7 (ebook)

© 2026 BookLife Publishing
This edition is published by arrangement with BookLife Publishing.

North American adaptations © 2026 Bearport Publishing Company. All rights reserved. No part of this publication may be reproduced in whole or in part, stored in any retrieval system, or transmitted in any form or by any means, electronic, mechanical, photocopying, recording, or otherwise, without written permission from the publisher. Bearport Publishing is a division of FlutterBee Education Group.

For more information, write to Bearport Publishing, 5357 Penn Avenue South, Minneapolis, MN 55419.

# Contents

What Is a Life Cycle?. . . . . . .4

Goats on the Farm. . . . . . . . .6

Getting Ready for Kids. . . . . .8

Mother's Milk . . . . . . . . . . 10

Cuddly Kids . . . . . . . . . . . 12

Joining the Herd . . . . . . . . 14

Billy Goats and Nanny Goats. . 16

All Grown Up . . . . . . . . . . 18

The End of Life. . . . . . . . . .20

Life Cycle of a Goat. . . . . . .22

Glossary . . . . . . . . . . . . . 24

Index . . . . . . . . . . . . . . .24

# WHAT IS A LIFE CYCLE?

All living things go through different stages of life. We come into the world and grow over time. Eventually, we die. This is the life cycle.

As humans, we start life as babies. We grow into toddlers and children. Then, we become teenagers. Finally, we are adults and get even older. We may have babies of our own, and then the cycle begins again.

# GOATS ON THE FARM

Animals on the farm go through life cycles, too. Farm goats are **domestic** animals. This means they are not wild. People keep them as **livestock**.

There are more than 200 different **breeds** of goats.

A group of goats is called a herd. Some farms have only a few goats, while others have hundreds or even thousands. Farmers raise these animals for their meat, their milk, and their warm hair called wool.

# GETTING READY FOR KIDS

**Female** goats can have babies. Usually, a **pregnant** goat has two babies, called kids, growing inside her at a time. After about five months, the kids are ready to be born.

A PREGNANT GOAT

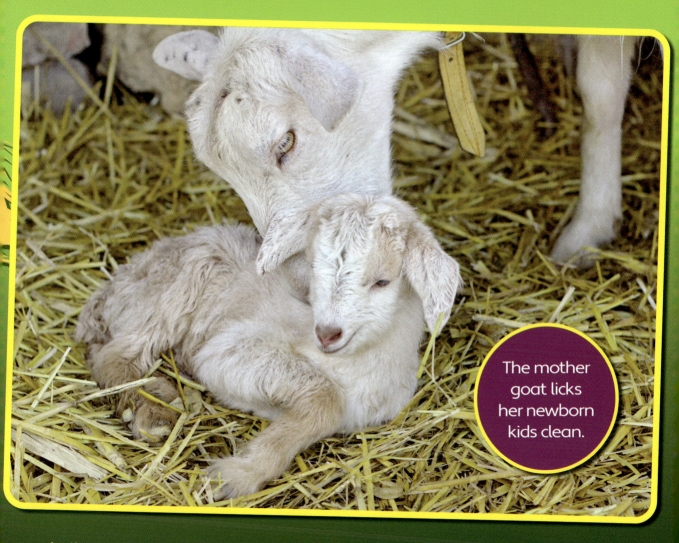

The mother goat licks her newborn kids clean.

When it is time to give **birth**, the mother goat finds a spot to be alone. Sometimes, she gives birth by herself. Other times, farmers may need to help get her kids out.

# MOTHER'S MILK

Kids drink milk from their mother's body soon after they are born. This milk gives the kids the **nutrients** they need to have a healthy start in life.

The mother goat makes milk in a part of her body called the udder.

UDDER

A mother goat's body can make milk for about 10 months after her kids are born. Often, there is more milk than her kids need. Farmers take the extra milk from the mother during this time.

# CUDDLY KIDS

The little kids are able to stand and walk soon after they are born. They may even run and jump on their first day.

A newborn goat can weigh up to 10 pounds (5 kg).

Baby goats and their mothers make sounds to **communicate** with one another. These sounds are called bleats. Kids can recognize their mother's bleats soon after they are born. A mother goat can recognize the bleats her kids make, too.

# JOINING THE HERD

Within a few weeks, kids start nibbling on grass along with drinking milk. After a few months, they switch to eating only solid food. Then, young goats can join the rest of the herd.

Goats can eat lots of different foods. But they usually munch on grasses and grains.

A goat may make a loud noise like a scream when it is alone.

Goats are very social animals. This means they live together in groups. They are close with other goats on the farm.

# BILLY GOATS AND NANNY GOATS

Male goats are called billy goats. Female goats are called nanny goats. Most breeds of goats grow horns. Usually, the males have longer horns than the females.

A BILLY GOAT

A NANNY GOAT

BEARD

Many breeds of goats grow beards under their chins. Beards are more common on billy goats. However, some nanny goats can grow short beards.

# ALL GROWN UP

Goats are considered adults when they are about six months old. However, they are still growing! For some breeds, fully grown goats can weigh about 250 lbs. (110 kg).

Nanny goats are often smaller than billy goats.

Most nanny goats are fully grown when they are about two years old. This is when many of them have their first kids.

# THE END OF LIFE

Goats have many **predators**, including foxes, wolves, and bears. Farmers may build fences and train other animals to keep their herds safe.

Dogs, donkeys, and llamas are often used to guard goats.

Goats can live for about 12 years. However, farm goats raised for their meat usually don't live this long.

# LIFE CYCLE OF A GOAT

A goat begins its life as a kid. Its mother licks the baby goat clean, and it quickly learns to walk. The kid drinks its mother's milk and grows bigger. Eventually, it becomes an adult.

KID

ADULT GOAT

During its life, a goat may have kids of its own. Eventually, the goat will die, but the kids live on and have even more goats. This keeps the life cycle going!

# Glossary

**birth** when a female has a baby

**breeds** different types of an animal

**communicate** to share information with others

**domestic** tamed for use by humans

**female** a goat that can give birth to young

**livestock** animals that are raised by people on farms or ranches

**male** a goat that cannot give birth to young

**nutrients** substances plants and animals need to grow and stay healthy

**predators** animals that hunt and eat other animals

**pregnant** when a female animal has babies growing inside her

# Index

**beards** 17
**bleat** 13
**farm** 6-7, 15, 21
**horns** 16

**kids** 8-14, 19, 22-23
**meat** 7, 21
**milk** 7, 10-11, 22

**predators** 20
**social** 15
**wool** 7